Selected original photographs

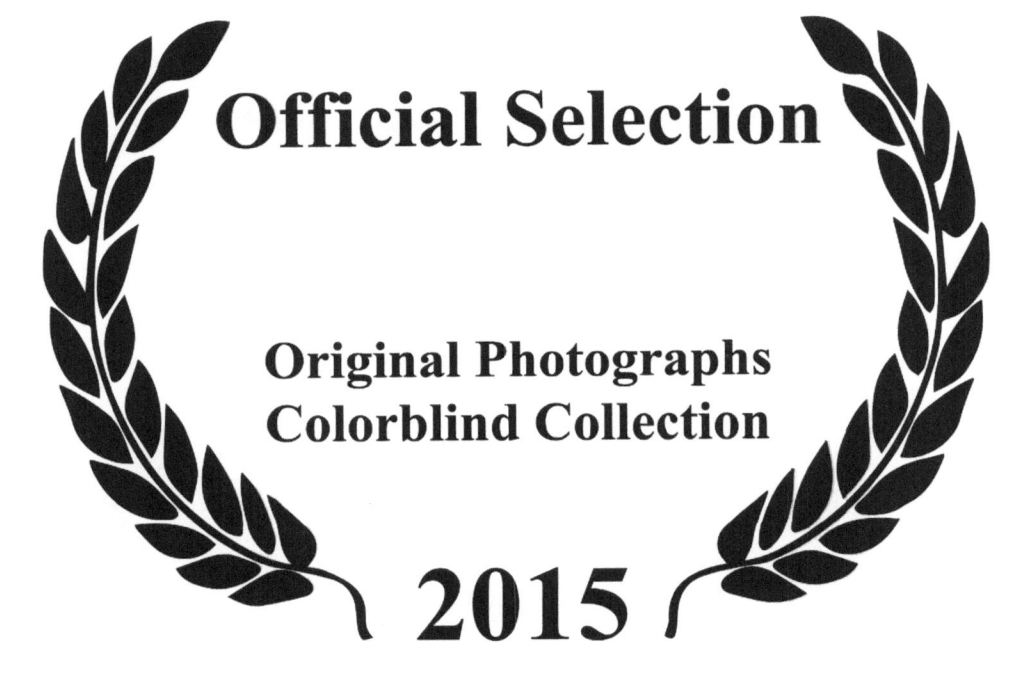

Official Selection

Original Photographs
Colorblind Collection

2015

Joseph Fleming

Colorblind Black & White
photography portfolio

Decades of being around accomplished talent producing absolutely phenomenal quality work has taught that we are capable of greatness. It is possible to meet our destiny and become it. Experiencing excellence done with such apparent ease and humble selfless gratification is the motivation for this photography. Most important was having the freedom.

Being colorblind gives an advantage when composing black & white… less confusion.

These selections, from thousands of captures during years of travels, exhibit the lonely freedom of a hidden perspective. All images were framed in the camera and presented without edits, genuine as seen through the lens. Panchromatic conversion applied by unique proprietary process.

Original fine art and custom work available.

info@ BEACHNOISE.com

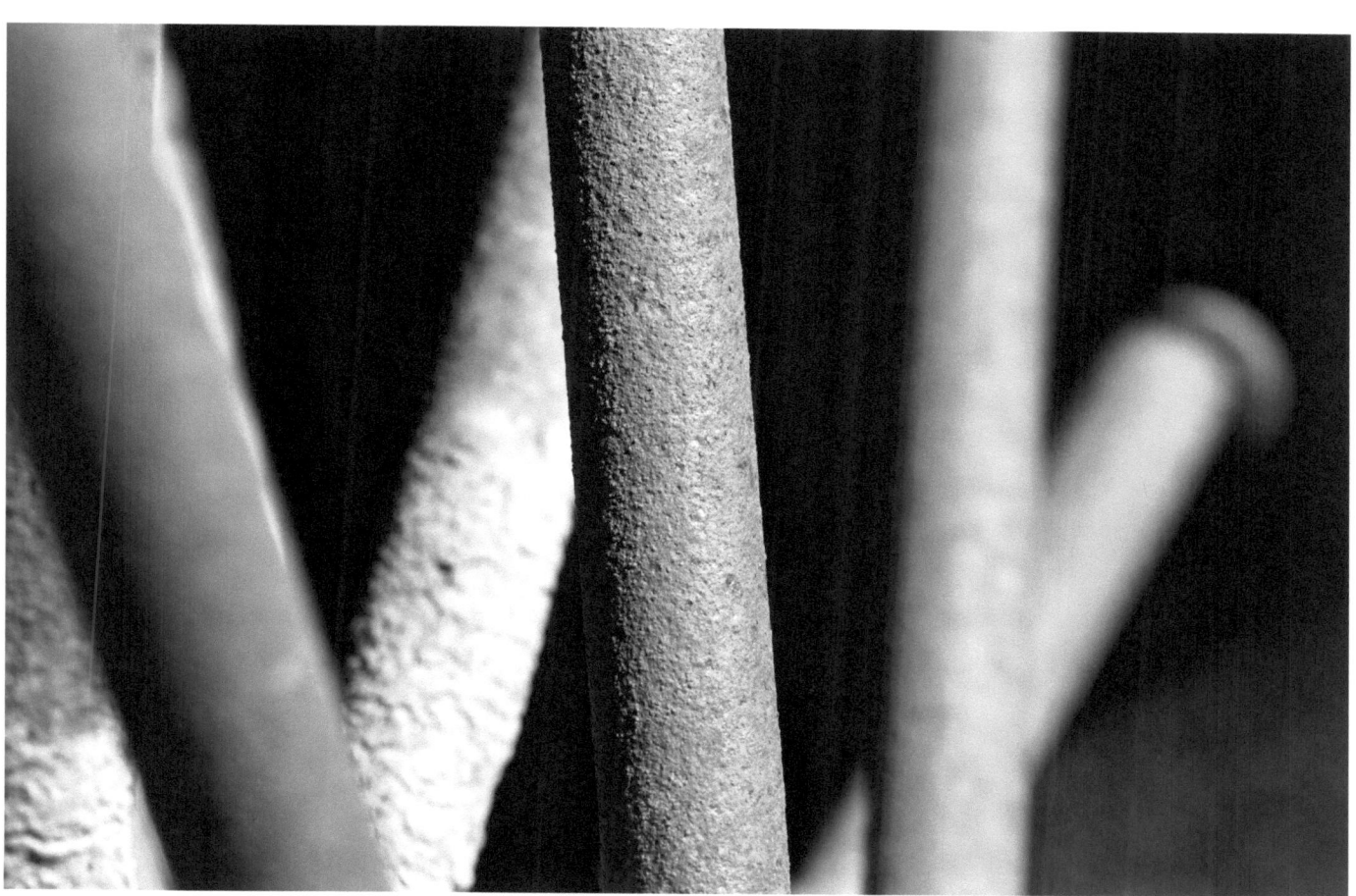

0780

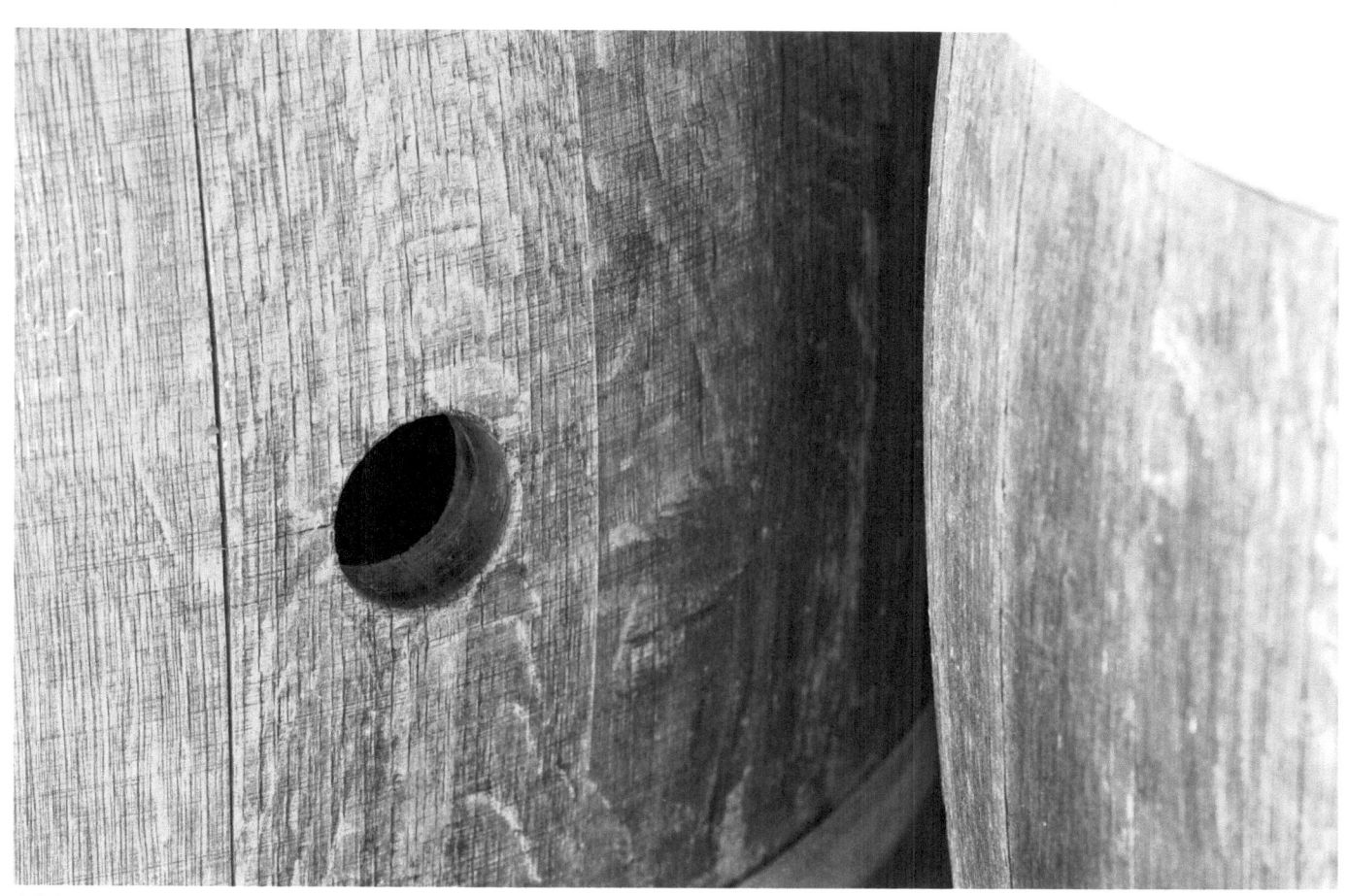

0826

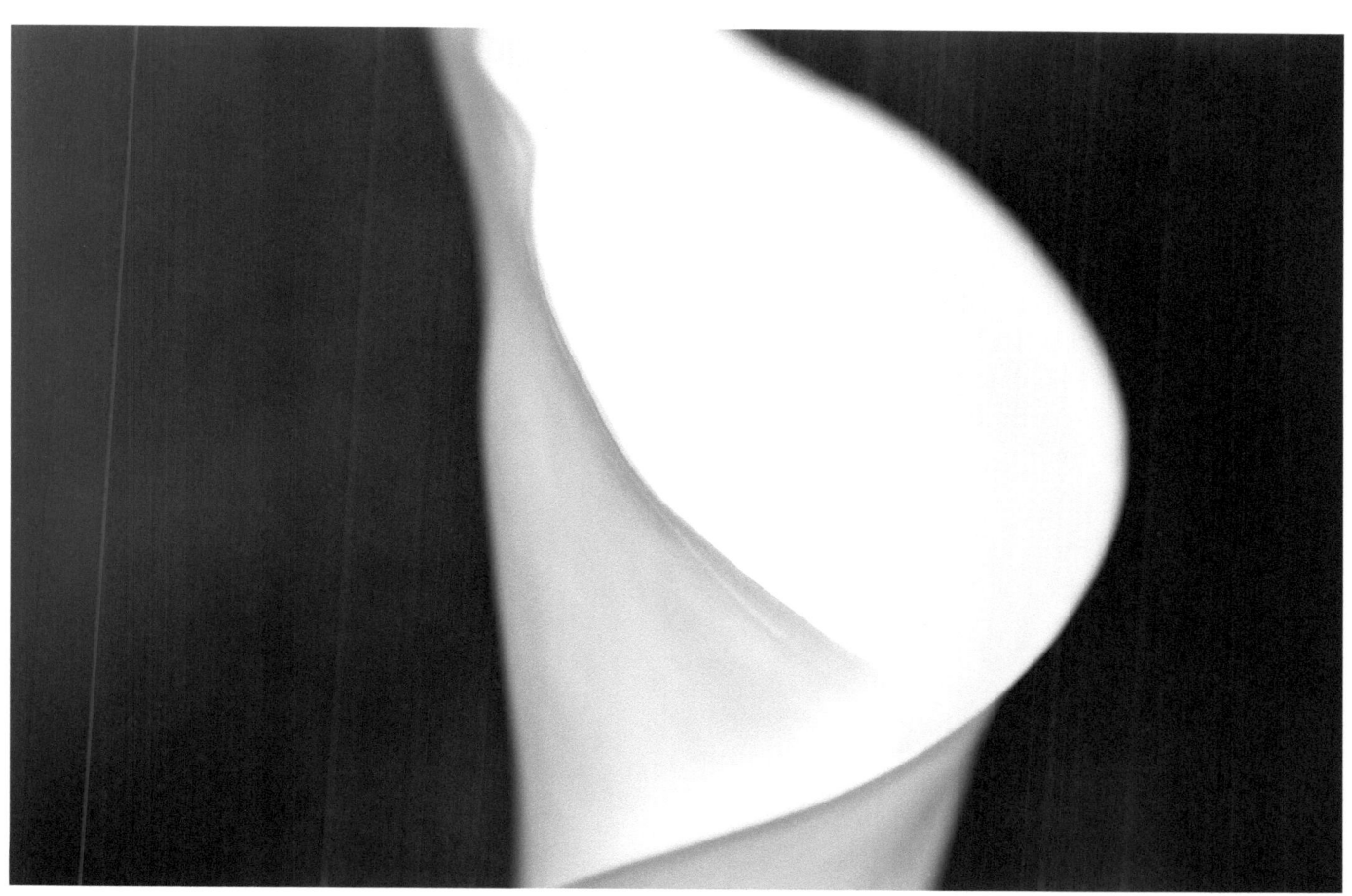

0920

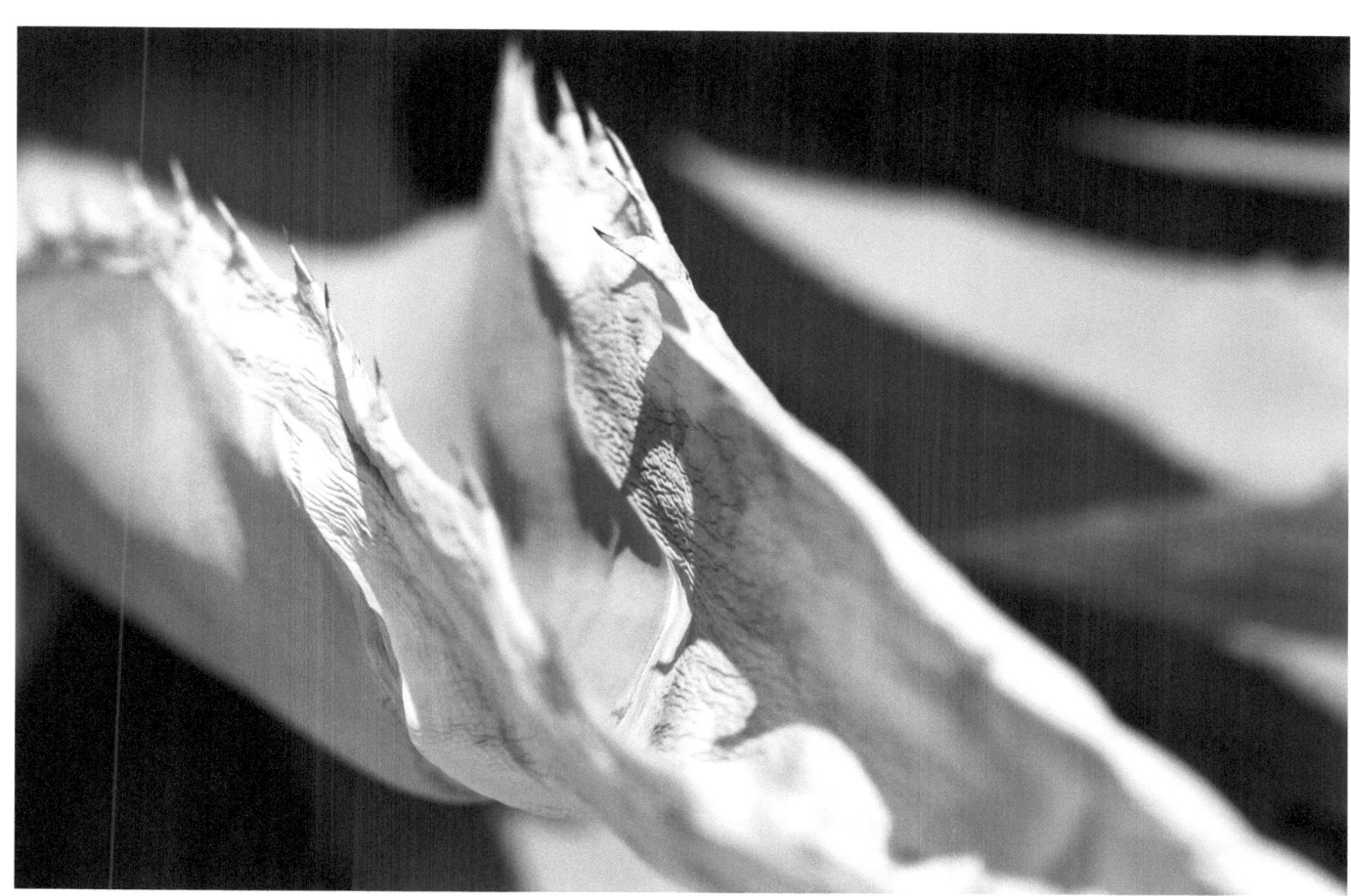

1581

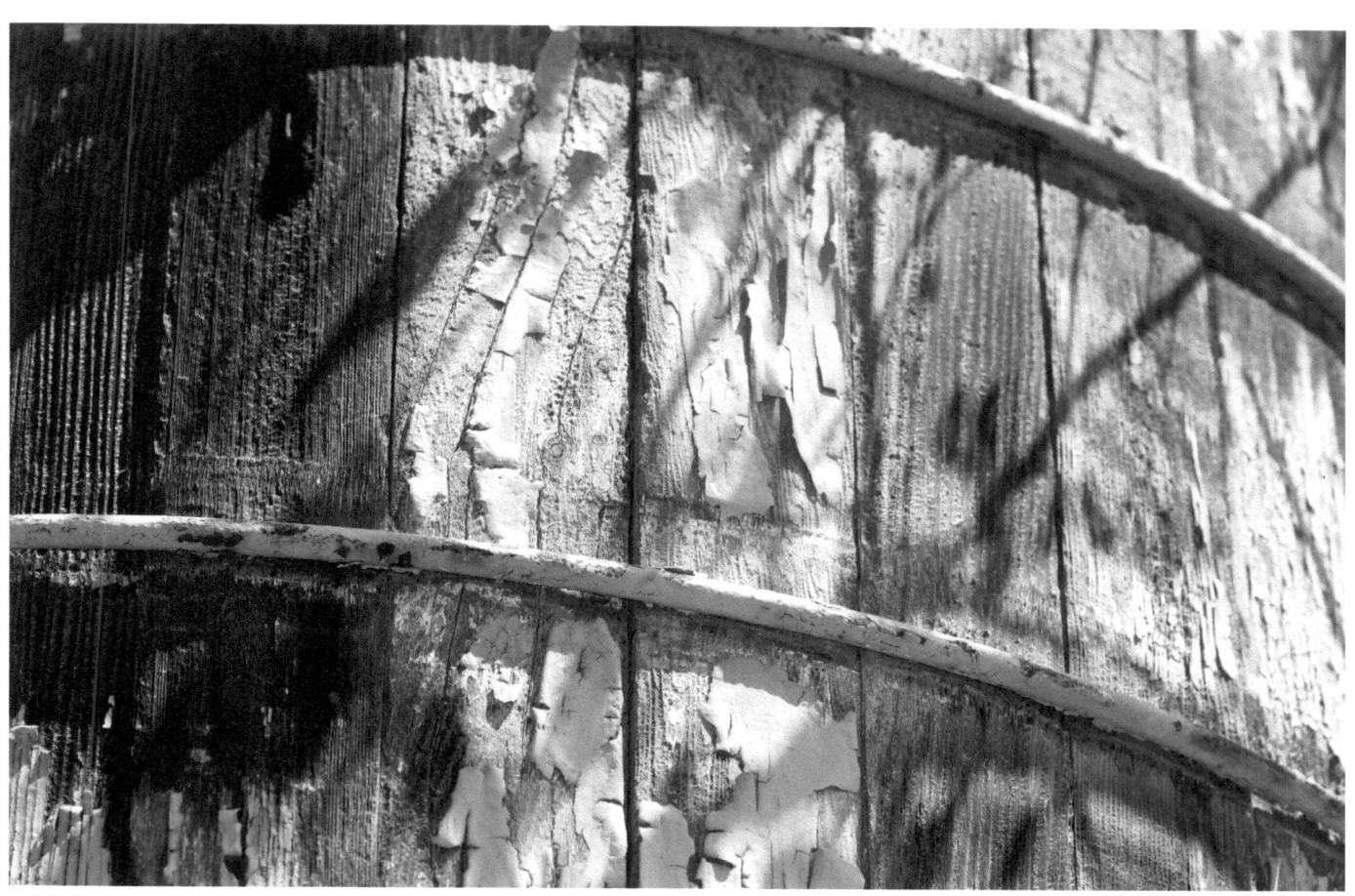

1608

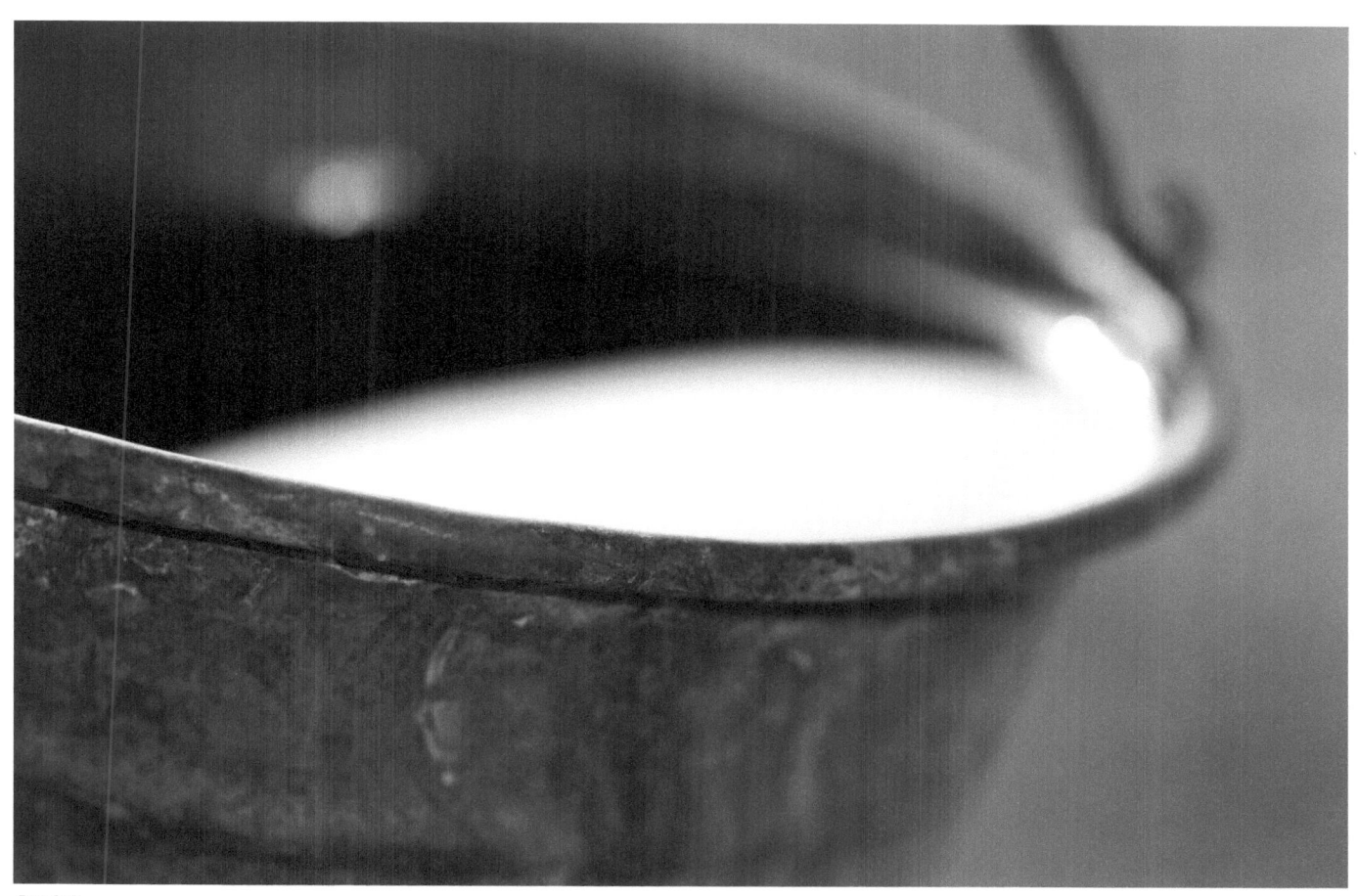

2180

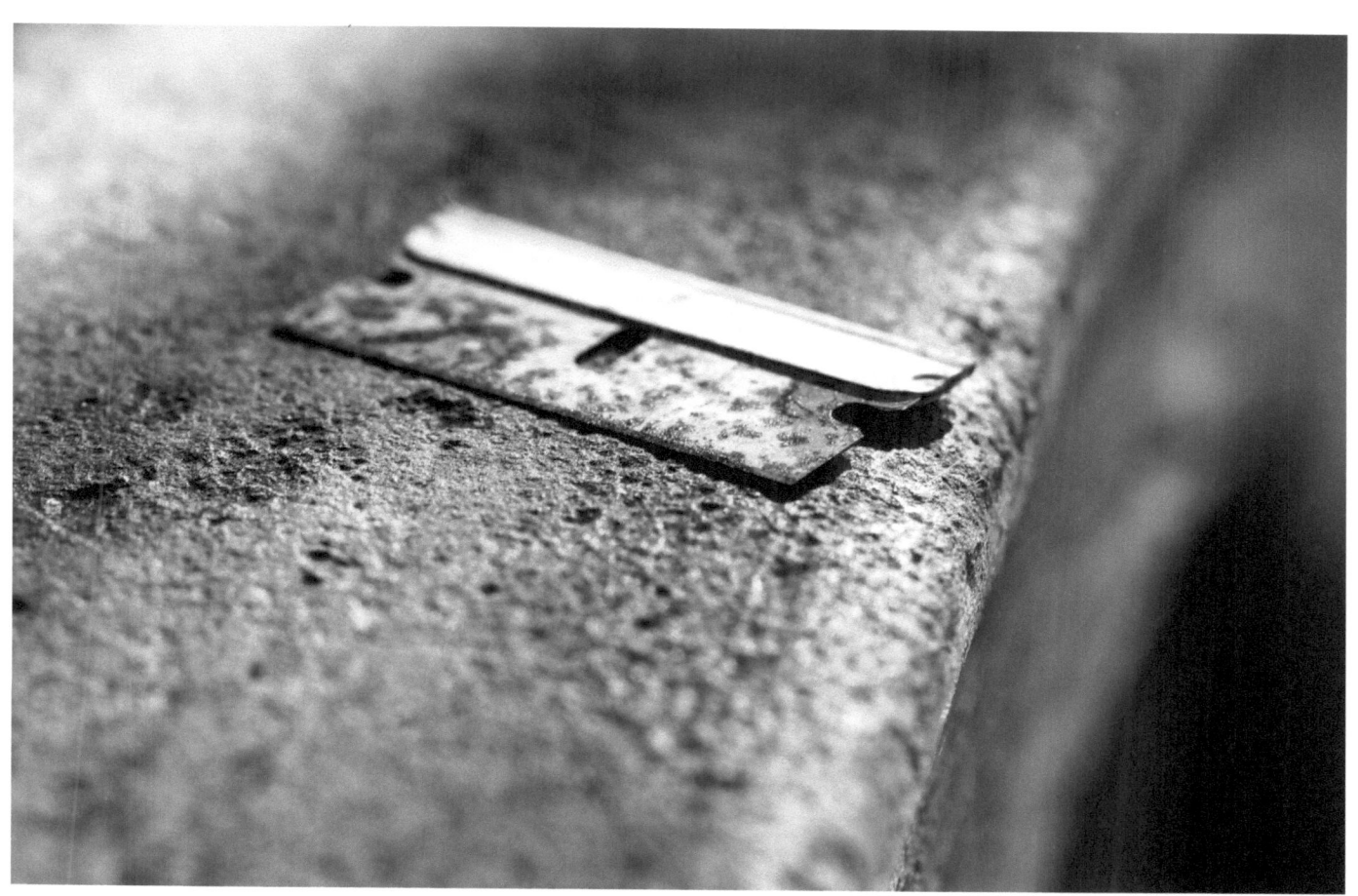

2467

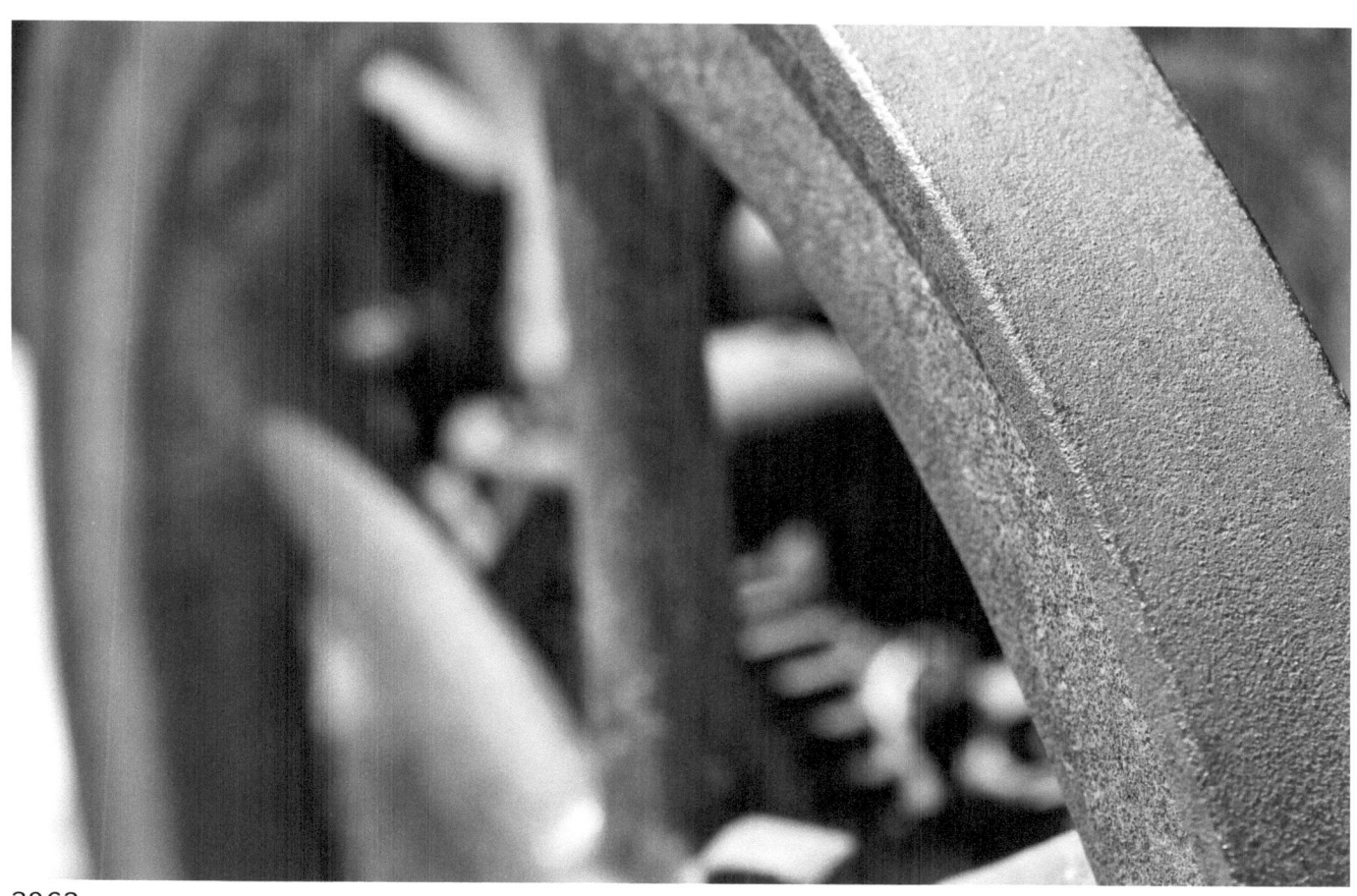

2962

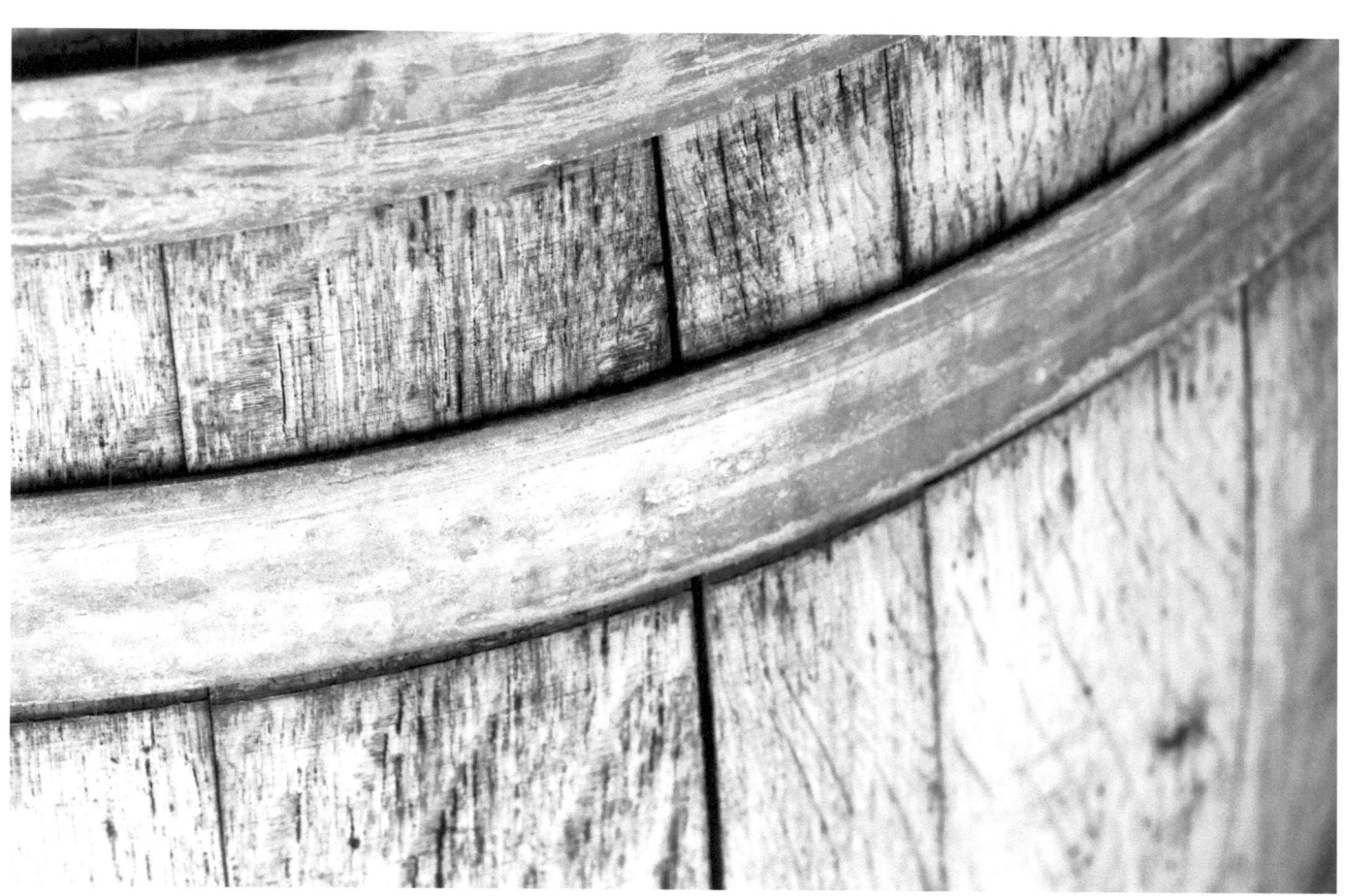

3151

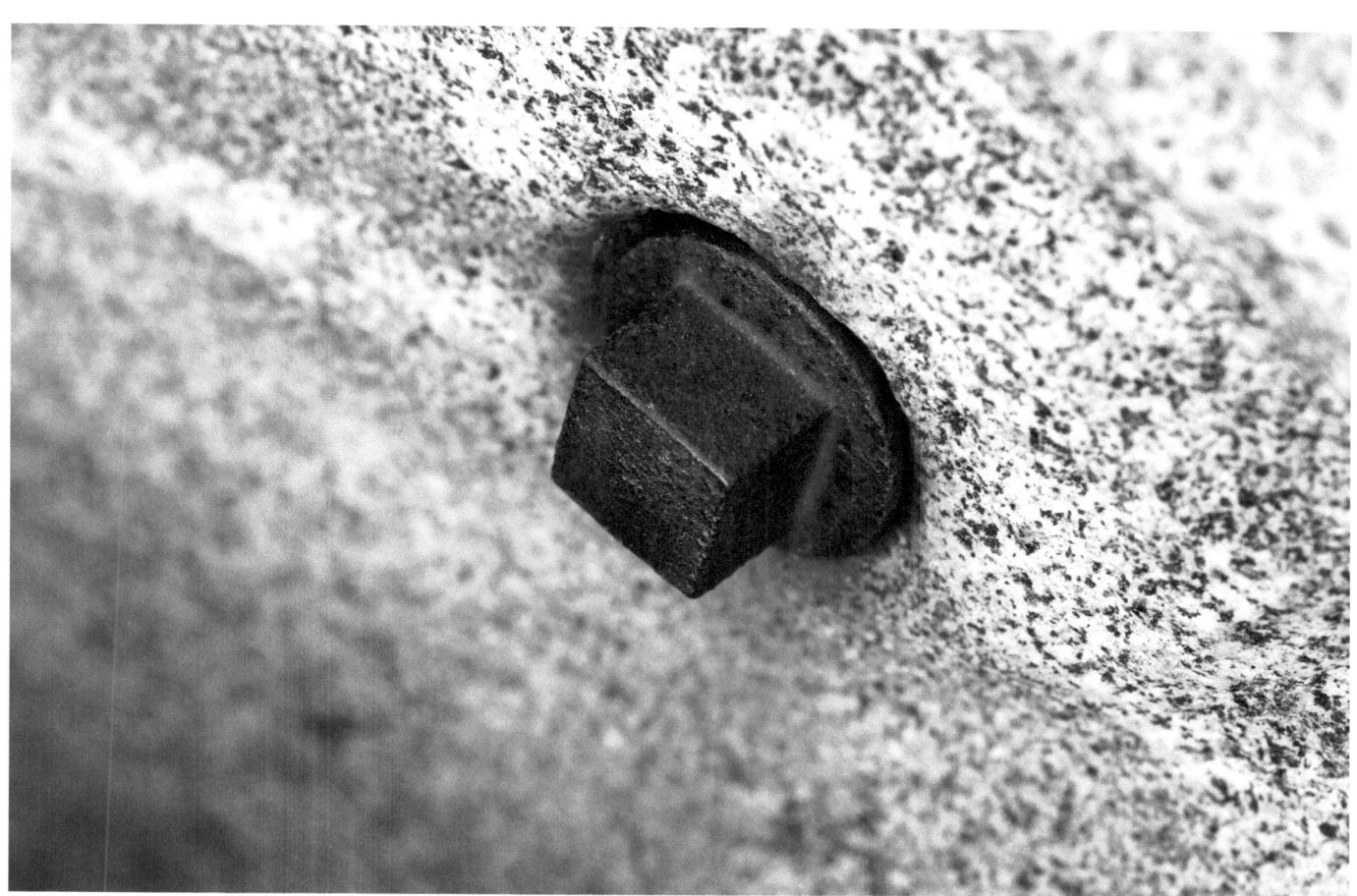

4035

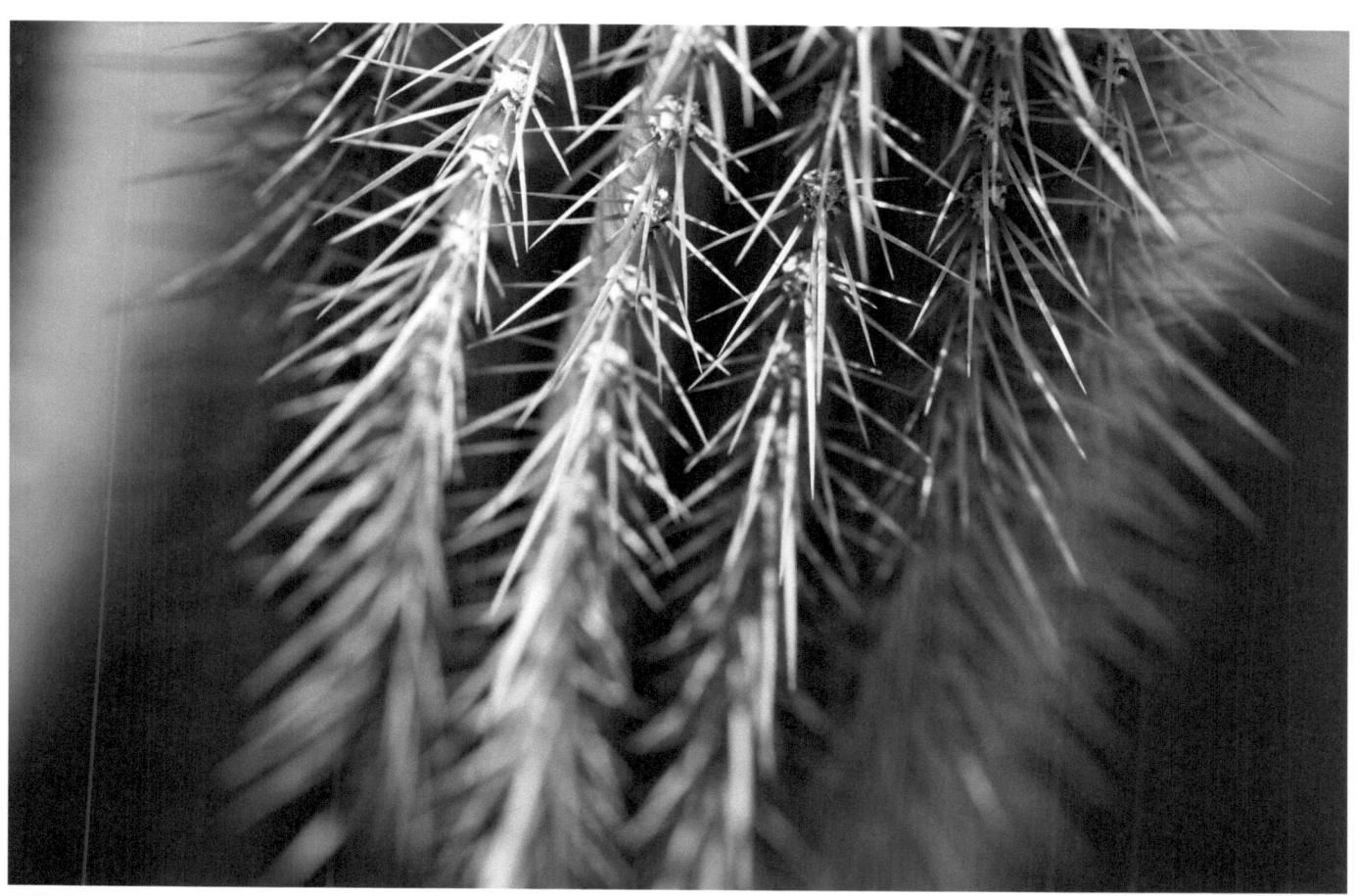

4070

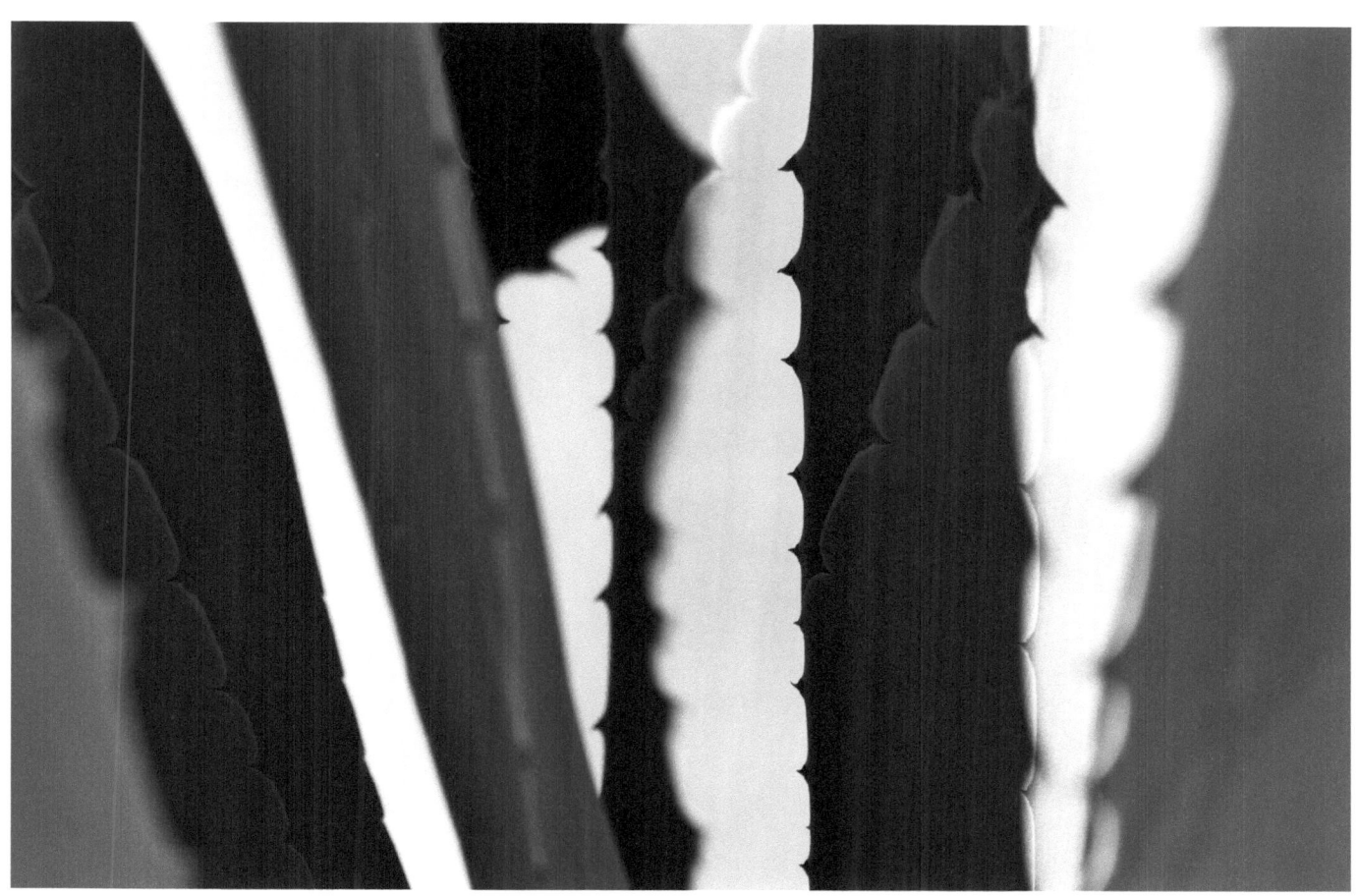

4099

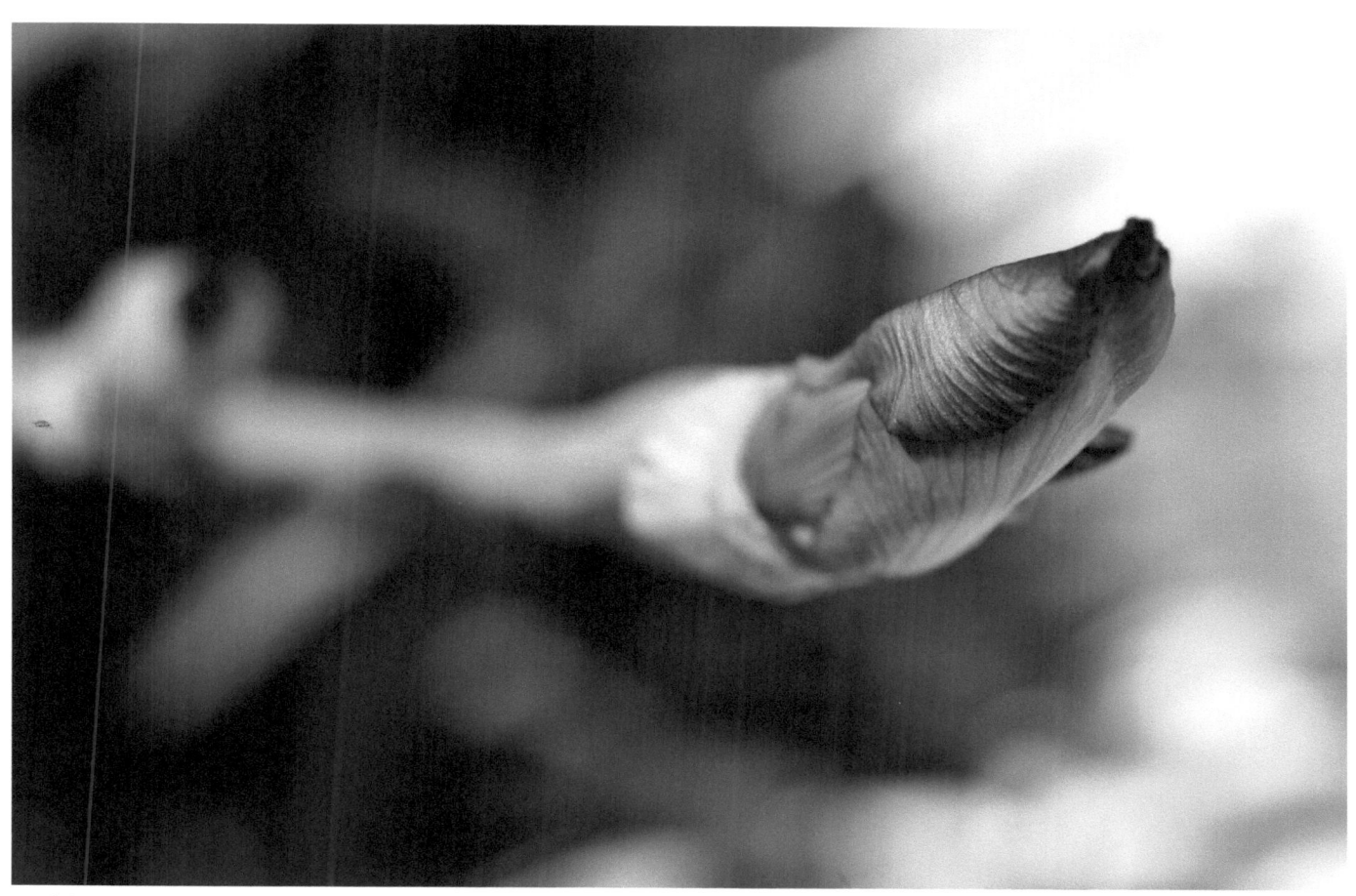

5492

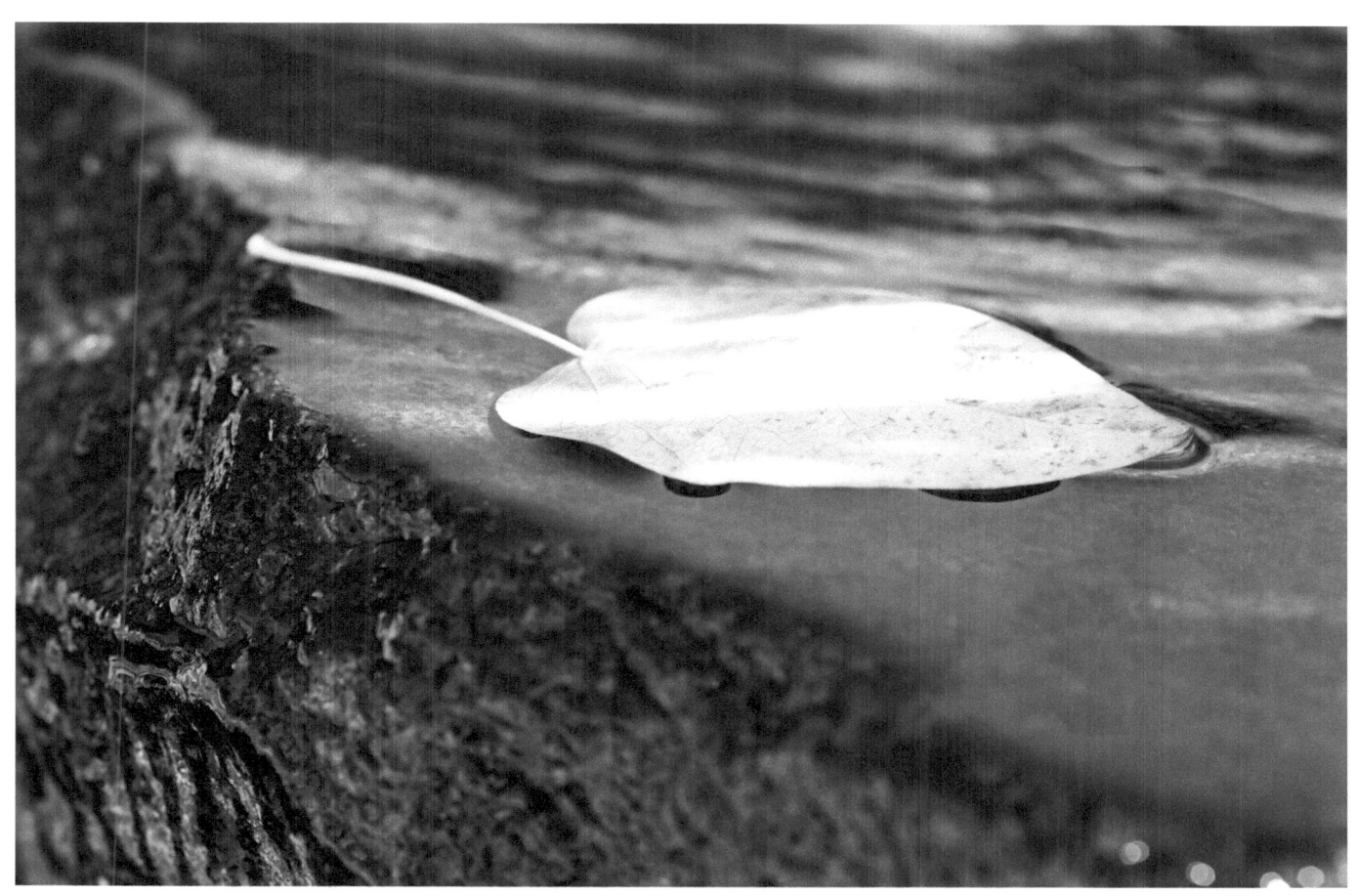

5750

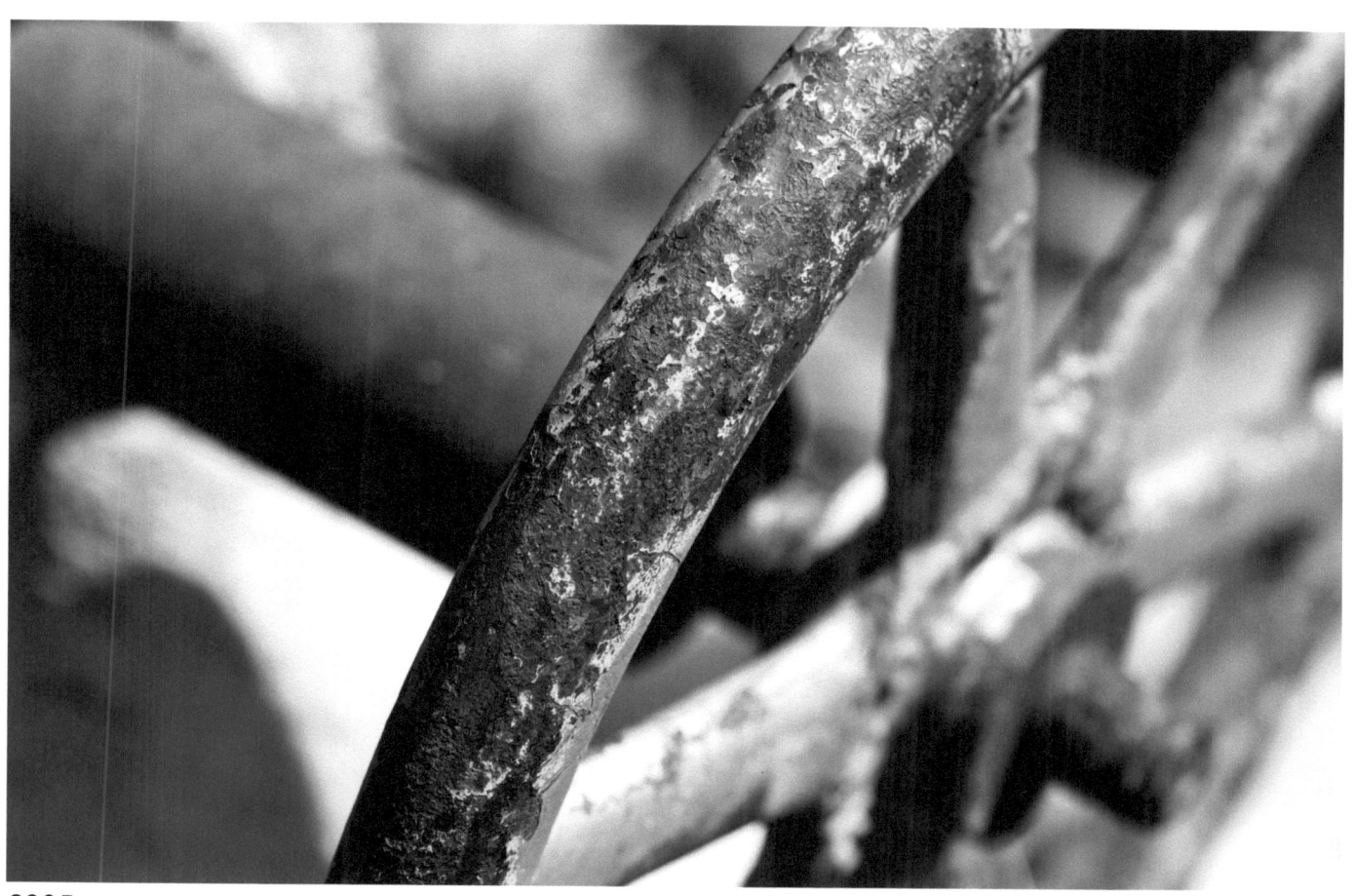

6095

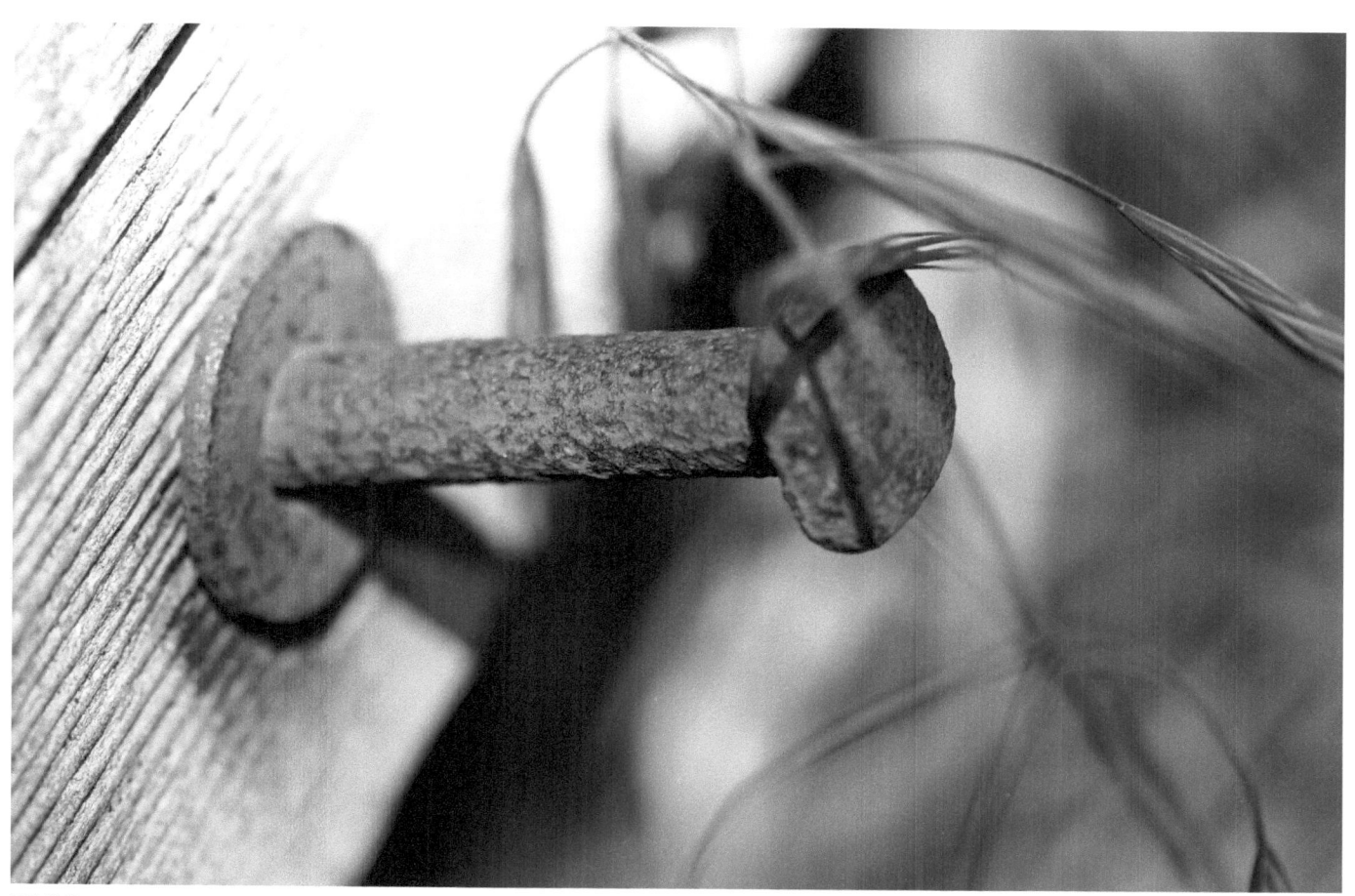

7182

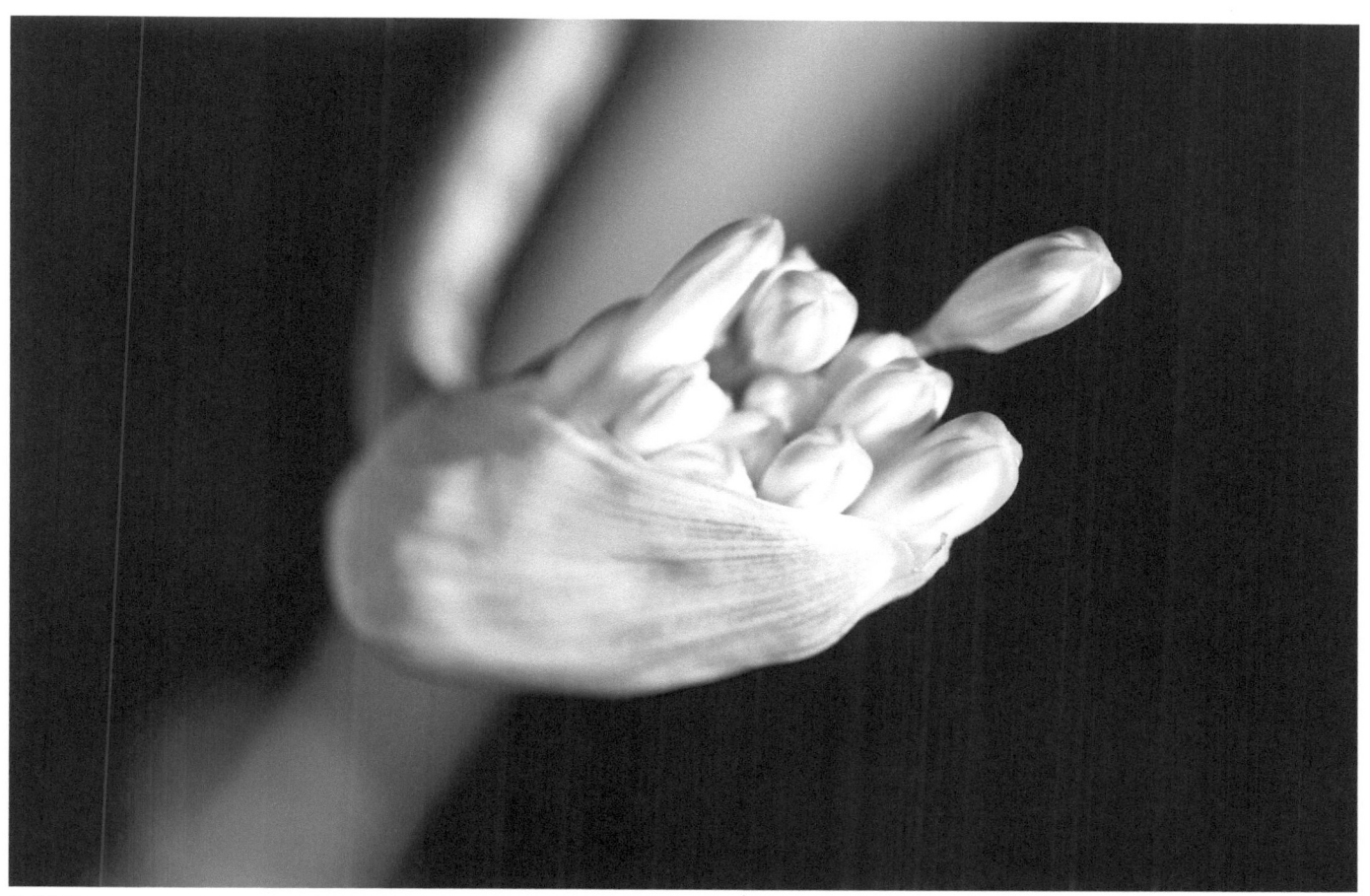

8407

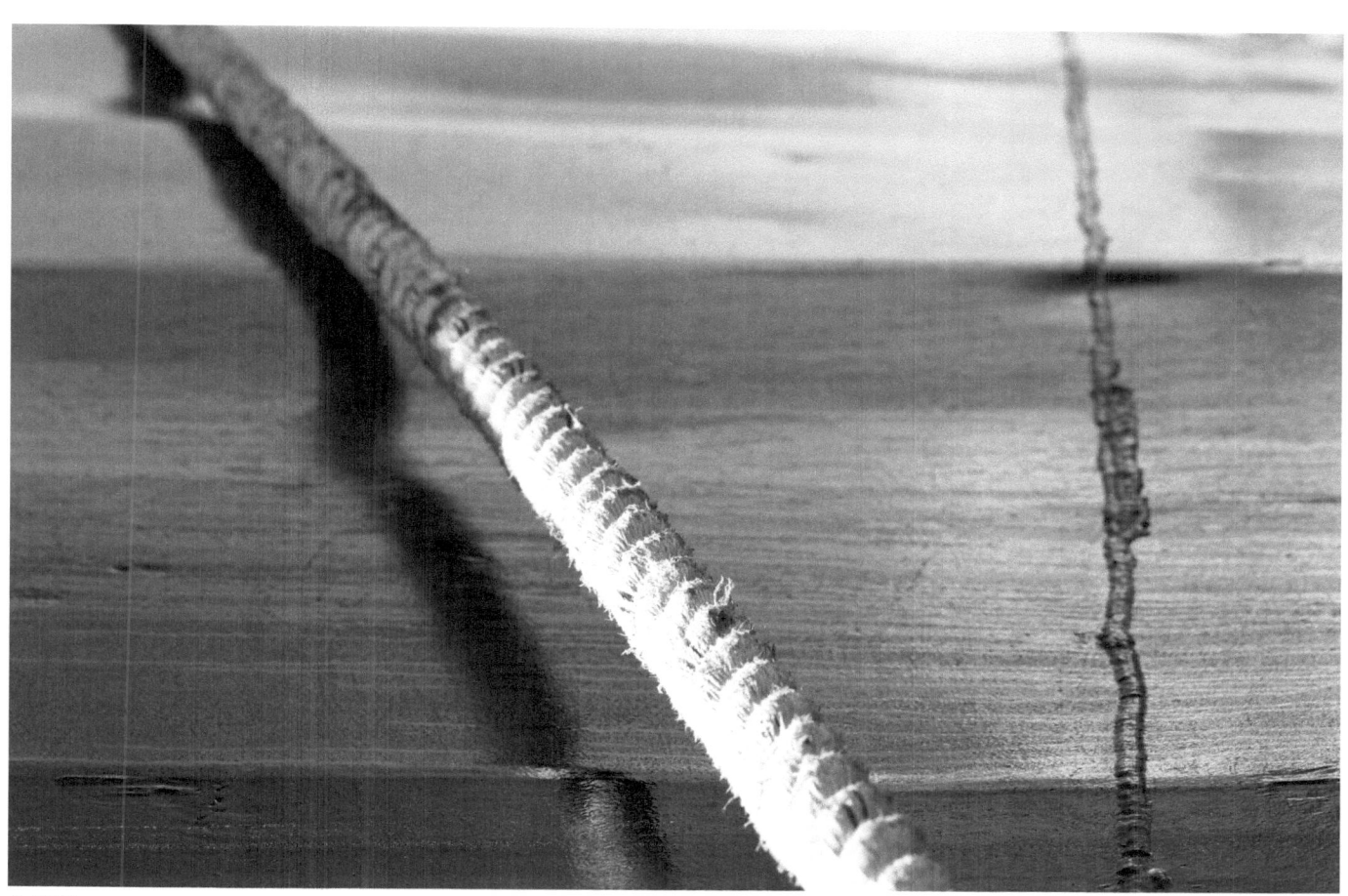

8470

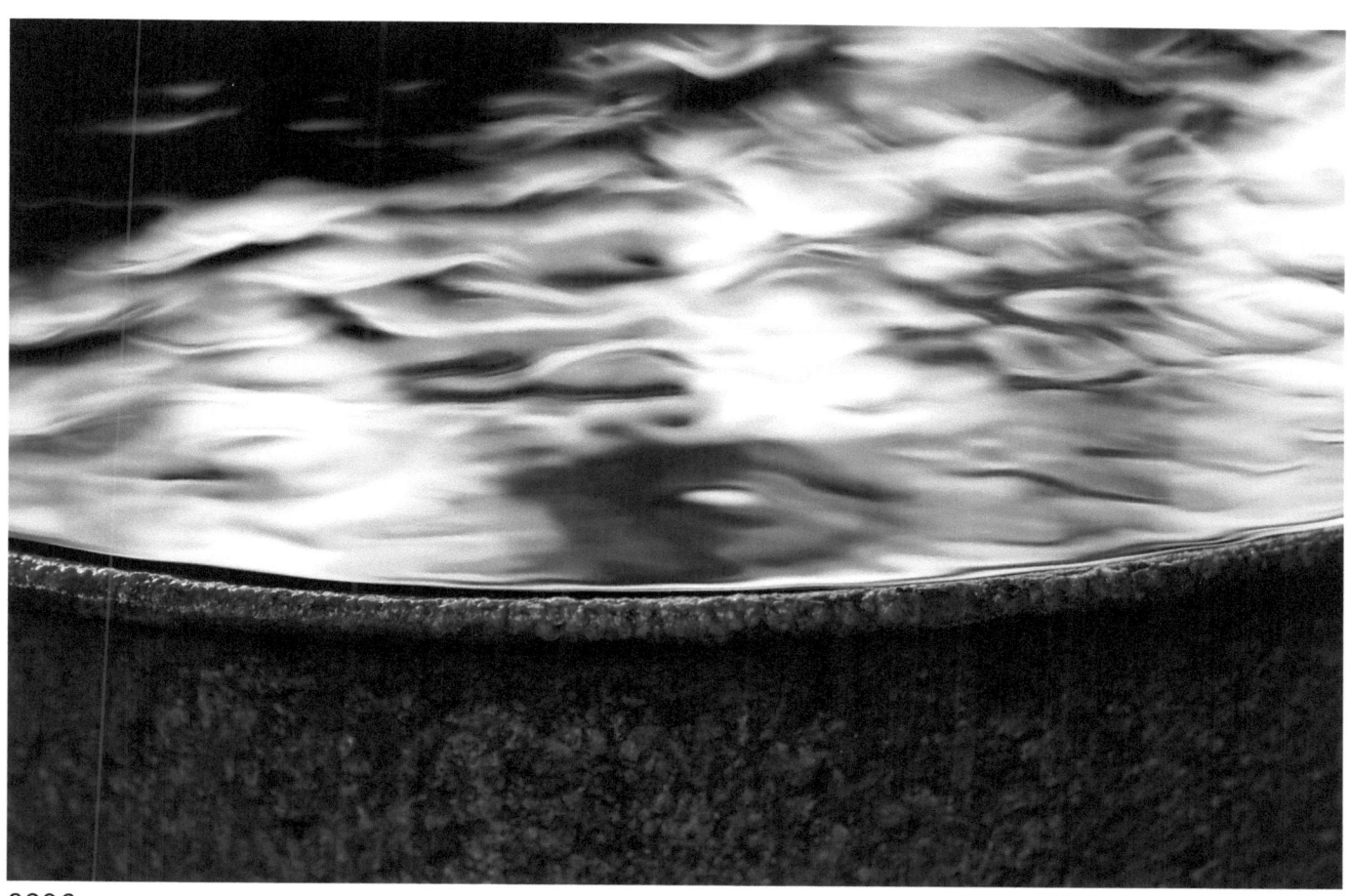

8896

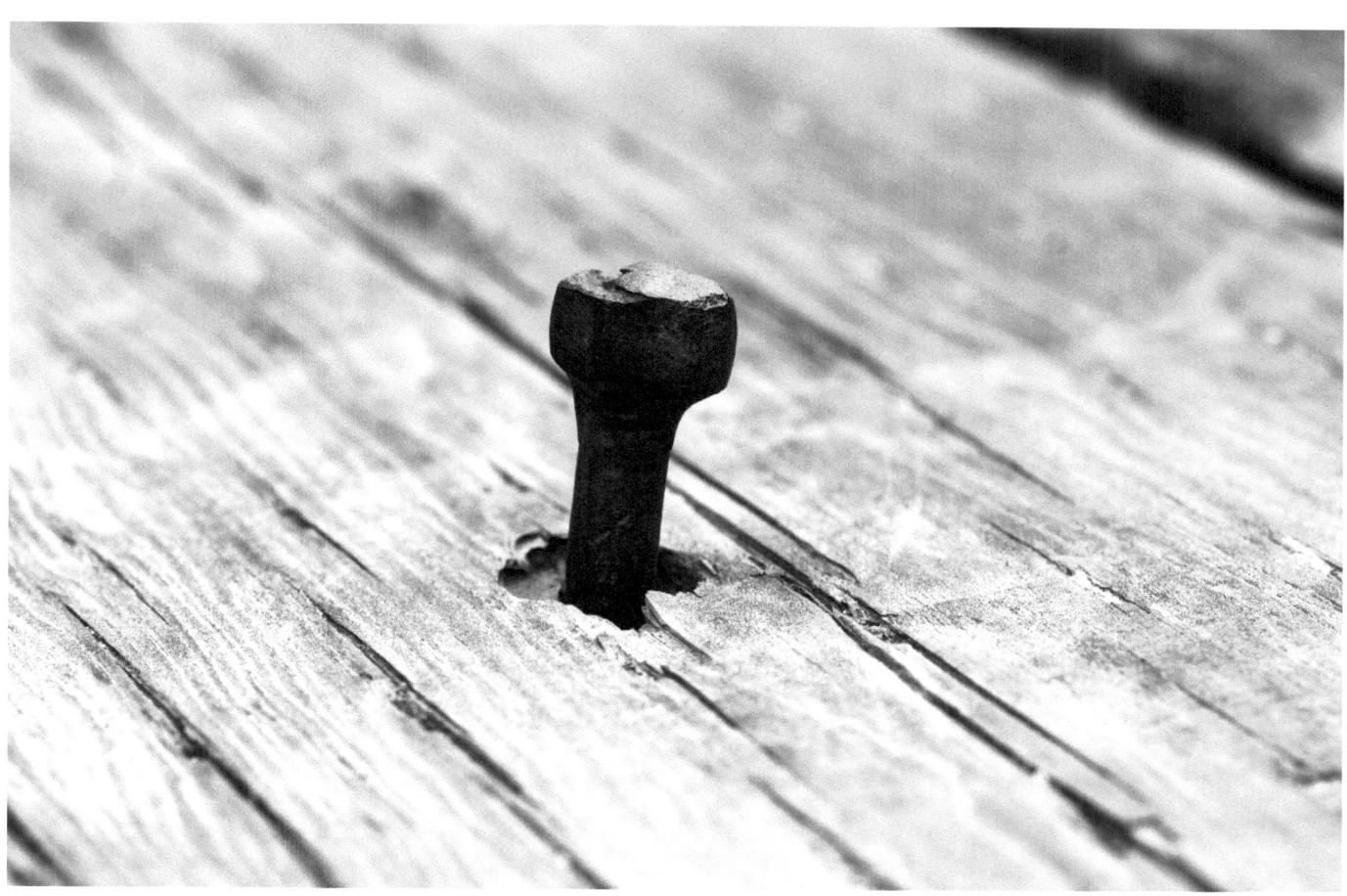

9024

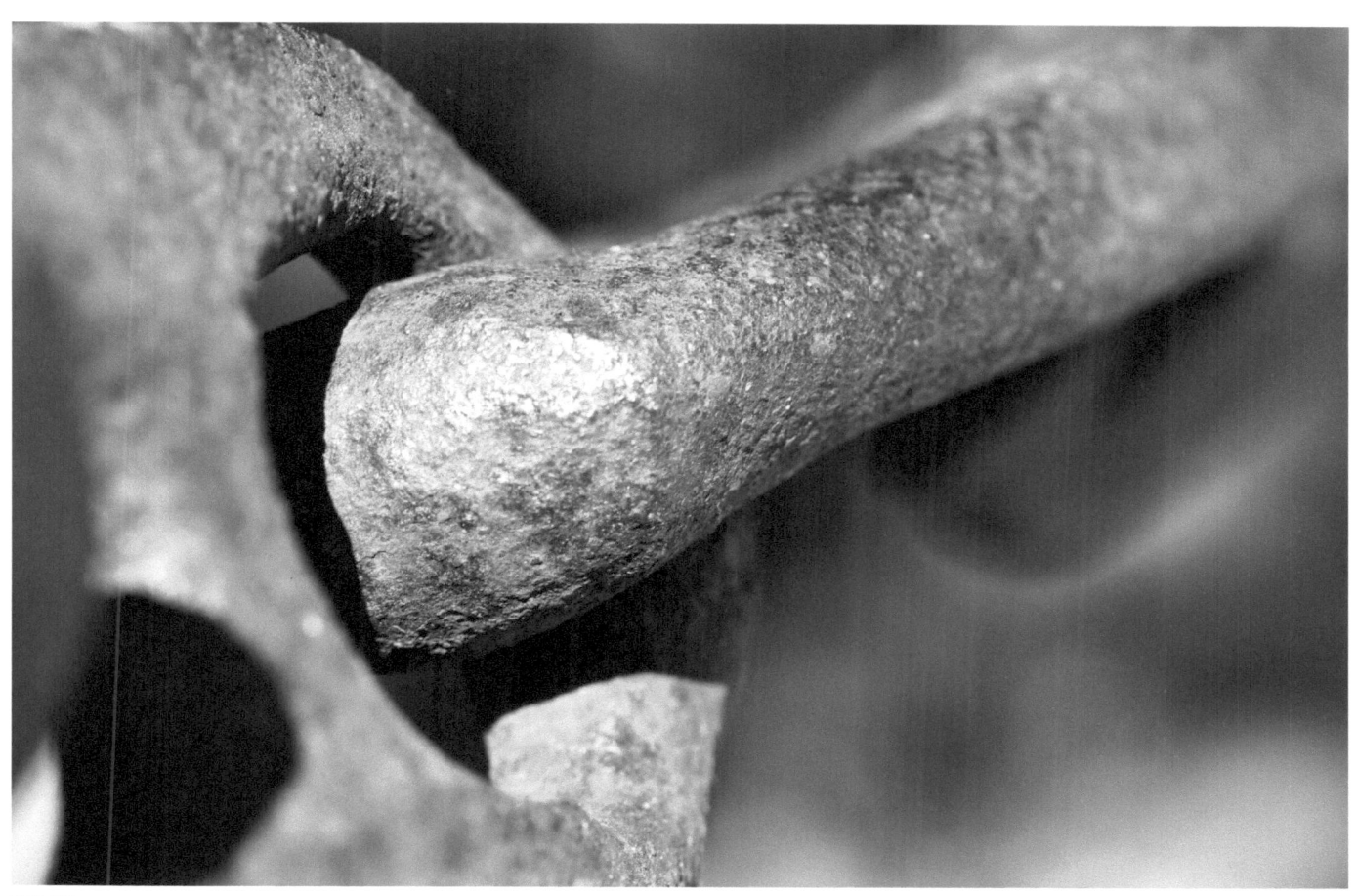

9353

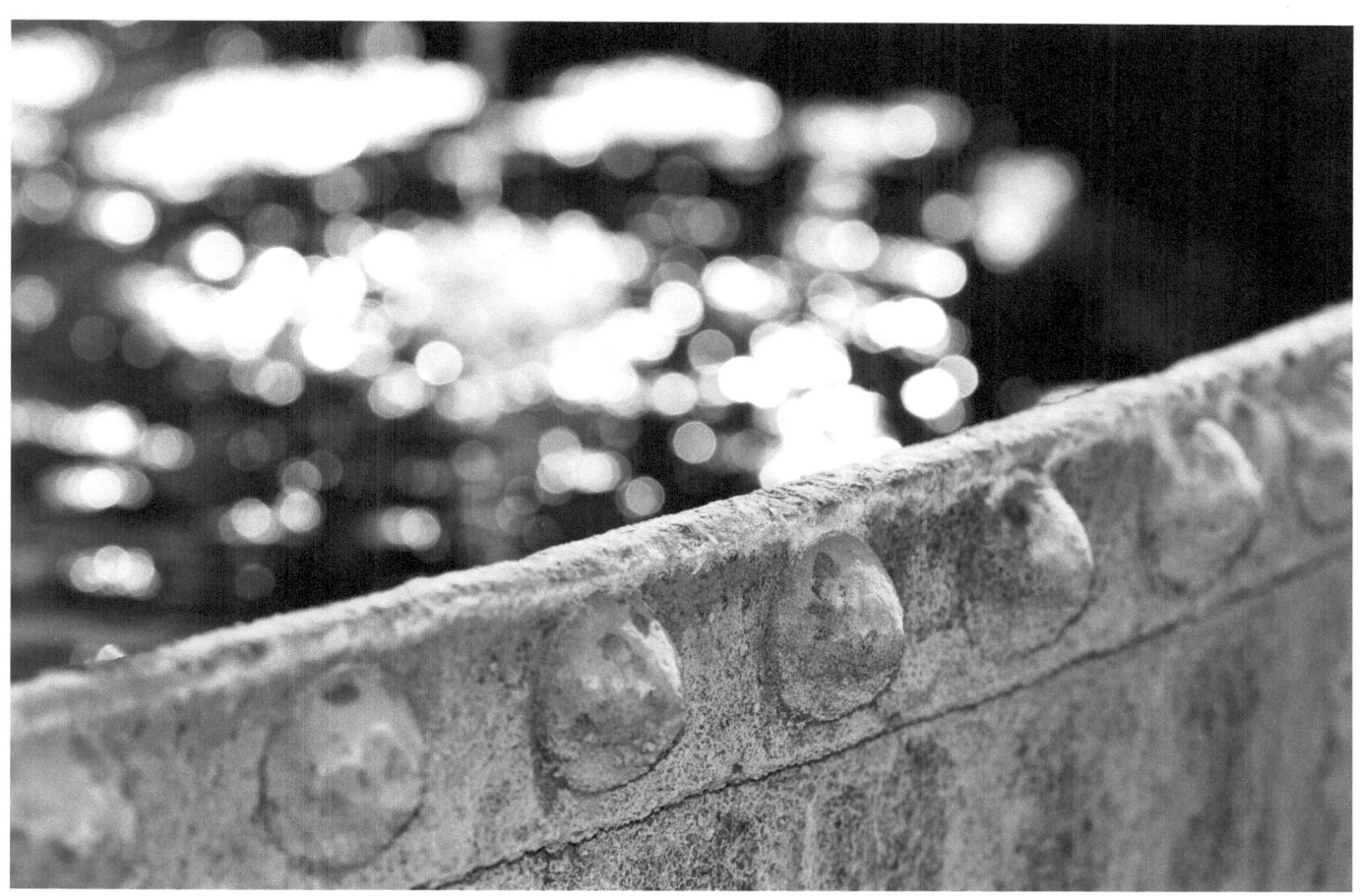

9430

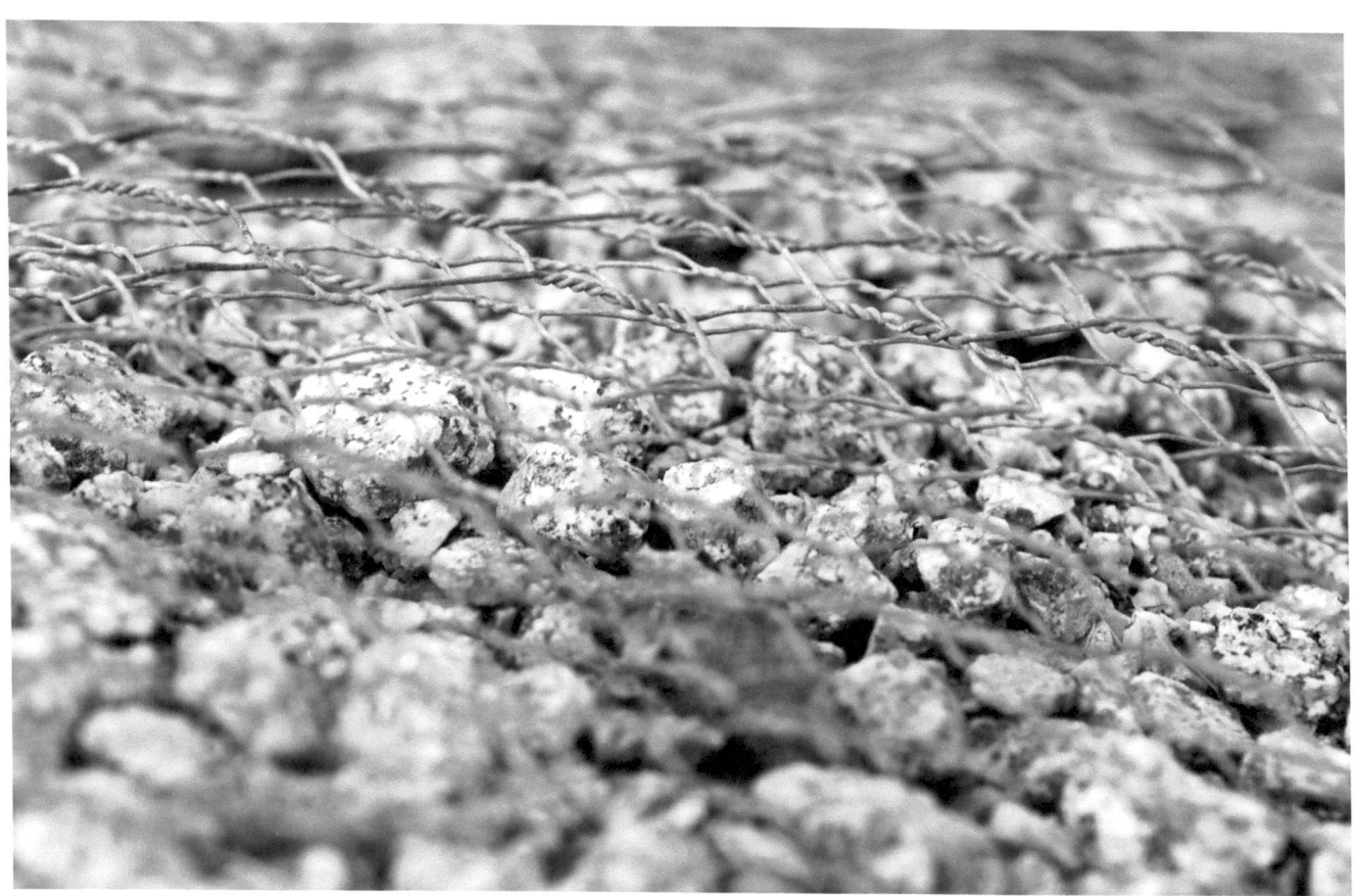

9970

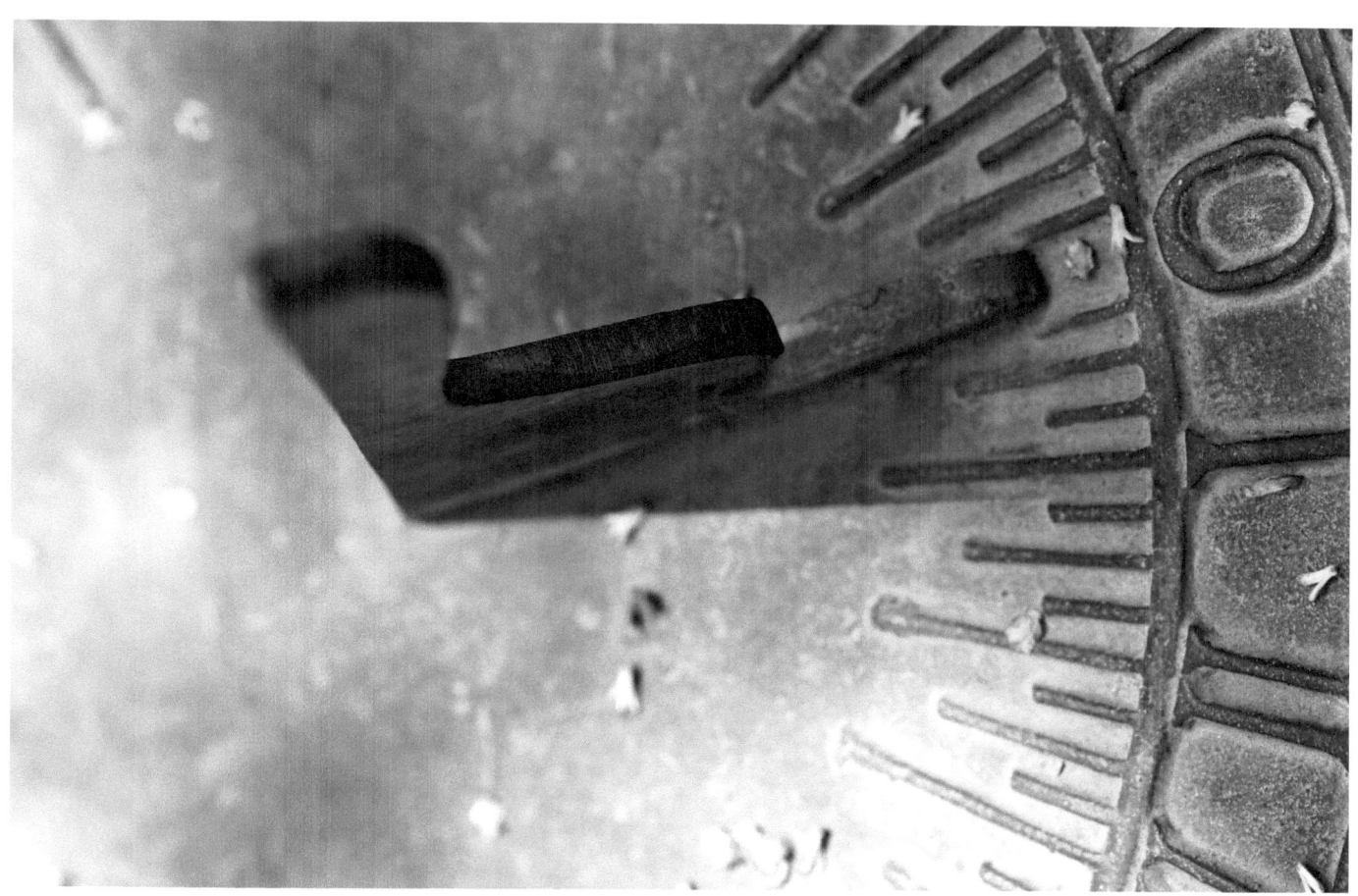

10002